MW00761280

Faith [2.1]

You Can Do More Than Just Believe

GAMAL T. ALEXANDER

Watersprings
PUBLISHING

FAITH 2.1
Published by Watersprings Publishing, a division of
Watersprings Media House, LLC.
P.O. Box 1284
Olive Branch, MS 38654

Printed in the United States of America.

Library of Congress Control Number: 2019937939

ISBN: 978-1-948877-18-3

Table of Contents

Dedication

Kindergarten taught me the importance of using the magic words "please" and "thank you". Well, this is the page where I get to use some of the magic that I've learned...

Thank you to the special people with whom I've been blessed to share this journey. Whether it was a gentle rebuke, consistent encouragement or a tangible gift, I could never really repay you. You know who you are. You have done everything in your power to help me bring this idea to life! You saw this in me before I ever did and refused to let it die. I salute you.

Thank you to the family I was given...Dad, siblings, etc... I won the lottery with you guys.

Thank you to the family I have chosen (aka my friends). I couldn't have chosen better if I tried.

Thank you to the faith community that allows me to serve.

Thank you, my Lord who continues all my faith, to grow.

Thank you all!

Now please, If I've omitted anyone, charge it to my head and not my heart.

And to the reader... please enjoy this book! Please and thank you...

GTA

Introduction

If I had to take a guess at one of the few things that just about everyone has in common, my guess would be our inclination to believe. It seems as if we all believe in something. Whether it be a higher power (research suggests that most Americans believe in something bigger than themselves), of the reliability of scientific evidence, or whether we simply believe in ourselves and the possibility for good in the world, the one thing we seem to share is that we all believe in something. We're inclined to believe. Almost driven to believe. There's something about our nature that just about makes it mandatory. There's something about our makeup that makes belief almost impossible to escape. We can't help ourselves. Our literature tells stories about those who believe. Our movies celebrate those who believe. Belief seems to be everywhere we turn. Testaments to belief are everywhere we go. One person believes that children are our future. "Another one believes they can fly". Another still believes in something "even if it means sacrificing everything." Either way, belief is not hard to come by.

God invites us to believe. God also wants us to know however, that belief is not all there is.

For the next 21 days I would like your permission to challenge your ability to believe and hopefully make you uncomfortable with the idea that believing is enough. For those who identify themselves as people of faith, I propose that God is extending an invitation to enjoy a connection with Him that includes much, much more. Beyond believing, God desires that we deepen our relationship with Him. God is, in fact, divine and "wholly other". Yet God wants to reveal Himself as our strength and source, shield and security, strong tower, sufficiency and salvation all rolled into one. God can be our everything! But in order to occupy that space in our lives, He must first make room in our hearts and minds. We must leave the edges of our faith experience behind and wade into the deeper waters of a meaningful, powerful, relationship with Him.

This powerful connection can be yours. All of God's abundance belongs to you...but you must do more than just believe.

Day 1

The Only Way

"By faith the people passed through the Red Sea as on dry land; but when the Egyptians tried to do so, they were drowned." Hebrews 11:29 (NIV)

Since when is walking through the sea with a wall of water on either side a good idea anyway?

I've honestly never stopped to ask myself that question until now, but it does give me quite a bit to think about. There you are, standing on the banks of the "Sea of Reeds" (While the "scholars" are busy debating whether or not "Red Sea" is an accurate translation, you and I are going to continue our discussion. No need to let a little disagreement get in the way of a good story. Deal? Deal. Now as I was saying…) On one side there are the mountains. Formidable and foreboding, they don't exactly represent the way forward, nor is there any easy way to get around. Like it or not, you have to respect the mountains. They aren't going anywhere.

On the other hand, there is Pharaoh and his army. He's pursuing you with the intent of capturing you and your people, and if he does, let's just say that he does NOT intend to talk. As a matter of fact, nothing about the weapons, infantry, or charioteers that have managed to accompany Pharaoh on his mission of retaliation suggest "let's talk this over as adults". He's not here for a conversation. Pharaoh is here for annihilation. Consider the mountains, and things don't look so good. Consider the army, and things go from bad to worse.

Now look around you. You have the most equipped, best trained, prepared army in the world chasing you and who's got your back? Let's just say you're not exactly surrounded by a team of crack commandos. And just so we're clear, they DO NOT have your back. They want to go back! This group of former slaves wouldn't know how to use a sword if you held their hands and swung it for them. They are huddled together for warmth, wondering if they're going to make it out of this desert alive. Except for the pillar of fire in front of them they have no protection from the impending disaster that's waiting in the desert sands. They are untrained. They are uncomfortable. They are unnerved. No one is quite sure what to do or what will happen next-including you. Suddenly, in the midst of the mayhem appears a miracle. At least, that's kind of what it looks like… The wind has been blowing all night and now a path appears. Straight through the sea. The water forms a wall on either side of the walkway as Moses, with his rod still outstretched, commands the people to go forward. Yes, forward. Forward is the only way. Forward is the only hope. Yet forward seems uncertain and unstable, downright terrifying. What prevents these walls from crashing down and drowning us? Who said this is the safest route anyway? Aren't we rushing things a bit? Couldn't we come up with a better, safer, more convenient solution if we just had a little more time? You're skeptical, and that's understandable. I can't say that I blame you. You have every right to be. I can just hear you now: "You're telling me that a God I can't see talked to the old man in front and told Him that we needed to walk across the ocean floor. Did I hear you correctly?"

Yes. Yes, I am. Now are you coming or not?

I'd be lying if I didn't admit that sometimes, the way forward isn't downright scary. I've had intense conversations with God where I've attempted to negotiate my way out of following His directions. "Do I have to?" "I don't understand!" "There has got to be a better way!" Chances are, you have had those conversations too. It's not that we don't trust God. Of course, we trust God. Who doesn't trust God? After all, He's God! He sees all and knows all and can do anything. He's beyond questioning, His rationale is beyond comprehension, and His power is beyond measure. Of course we trust Him. However, that doesn't prevent us from occasionally pausing, looking up to heaven and wondering aloud "You want me to go where?" "You want me to do what?" "You can't be serious". We mean no disrespect, but sometimes going forward looks and feels a lot like going through. Going through the heartache. Going through the disappointment. Going through the pain. It's only fair, we tell ourselves, that we look for an alternate route that doesn't look so ominous. After all, there has got to be a better way.

I've got news for you, there is no better way. That intimidating pathway through the sea will take faith to walk, but it's the only way- and the best way, because it's God's way. God said go forward and if God said go forward, you can be sure that He will walk beside you, stay behind you and lead you every step of the way. Even if those steps seem treacherous and lonely, you can go because God says go. The path through the sea seems like a bad idea, until God reveals that it's a "God idea". Then you move forward. Step by muddy step, you walk until you make it over to the other side.

When God leads, you go forward. No hesitation, no discussion. You go forward, because forward is the only way.

PERSONAL REFLECTION:

When is the last time you followed God and not been comfortable with where He was leading?

When the way God is leading makes you feel uncomfortable, how do you continue to trust Him on your faith journey?

Have you ever decided NOT to follow God because the way forward seemed uncomfortable? Do you have any regrets?

Who am I praying for?

What am I praying about?

PRAYER STARTER:

Faithful Father, I thank You for always leading me along life's journey. I realize that I have not always followed as I should, and as such I am grateful for Your patience with me. Forgive me for the times where I have not followed Your leadership in my life. I pray today...

_____

_____

_____

_____

_____

_____

_____

_____

_____

_____

_____

_____

_____

_____

_____

_____

_____

_____

– Amen

Day 2

When Anxiety Attacks

"Be anxious for nothing, but in everything by prayer and supplication, with thanksgiving, let your requests be made known unto God; and the peace of God, which surpasses all understanding, will guard your hearts and minds through Christ Jesus." Philippians 4:6-8 (NKJV)

anx·i·e·ty /aNG-zī-dē/ noun. A feeling of worry, nervousness, or unease, typically about an imminent event or something with an uncertain outcome.

Even if I didn't use Webster's dictionary to define it, you would have been able to describe anxiety. You would have described it in detail, given me pointers on how to handle it, and even passed along advice from your therapist or the last good book you read. Anxiety happens to be a familiar foe and an old friend all at the same time. Everybody knows what it feels like. Everybody's familiar with the damage it causes, and all the ways it keeps us from really living. Everyone has traveled past this life landmark at some point along the way. When it comes to anxiety, it's like the dentist chair. It's not my favorite place, but every responsible person will eventually have to pay a visit. We've all been there before.

We're human. There's no getting around that. No cutting corners. No talking your way into a more suitable arrangement. From now until our personal expiration date we will continue to be some variation of "human". We can improve ourselves and be better humans. We can educate ourselves and be more knowledgeable humans. We can take care of our bodies and be healthy humans. However, we will still be human beings nonetheless. Try as we might, the flaws and limitations that accompany the human condition will plague us in one form or another, forever. One of those limitations is the ability to predict and control the future. The alliance we form with tomorrow will always be uneasy. The unknown will always be our nemesis.

On one hand, our better angels tell us to leave tomorrow where it is. Why invest so much time and energy in something that can't be curtailed, conquered, or controlled? It makes no sense to lose sleep and gain gray hairs over calamity that has yet to come around. So why do it? It seems perfectly reasonable to live in the moment and stay out of the future- especially since you and I are only invited to partake of here and now. That seems reasonable, but it's not exactly doable. Not for most of us anyway. Not for those of us whose wheels are always turning and whose brains are constantly working overtime. Not for the single mother who is finishing her degree and feeding children and working a full-time job with no help on the horizon, and no rest in sight. Not for the ambitious graduate who wants to start her career off on the right foot. After all, the beginning of this journey is important. There are places to go and people to see. There are things to do and miles to go before you sleep. Don't worry? Tell that to the elderly who have worked their entire lives taking care of others only to be reminded that there is no one waiting at the end of life's rainbow with the pot of gold that will take care of them. For most of us, carefree carelessness is not an option. We think. We plan. We brood. We worry. Then we pray, turn our troubles over to Jesus, take our troubles back, and start the vicious cycle all over again. For us, anxiety is a constant companion, albeit an unwelcome, annoying one. That's just the way it is.

That may be the way it is, but the Bible tells us that this is not the way things have to be. While we sink further into our anxieties, God offers us the life preserver of His peace. In the face of our anxiety God expressly commands "Don't be anxious about anything". Clearly God's plan for our mental health is very different from the rest of society's. Our world says, "Manage your stress". God says, "I don't want you to worry at all".

So how exactly am I supposed to pull that off? I've already established that I'm human and as such, I have a natural inclination towards fretfulness. Don't worry? I could try, but I've got bills to pay and a promotion to secure and a degree to earn and money to make and kids to raise and… The causes of my anxiety run on even longer than the previous sentence. I'd love to evict worry and replace it with peace, but squatters' rights are hard to get around. Still, God has an answer. Rather than bury our heads in life's sand, God invites us to rest in Him. Don't dwell on your circumstances, but rather "Make your request known unto God". Believe it or not, it really is that simple. Ask God by faith, then let it go. After all, if God is going to move it, then why are you tackling it? If God is going to solve it, why are you still trying to figure it out? Faith only allows for one problem solver at a time, and God is so much better at solving life's problems than we are. Be anxious for nothing. Don't worry. Don't be discouraged. Don't be disheartened. Don't be dismayed. Ask God, then let it go. Live your life in God's peace. You're His child. That's the way it ought to be.

PERSONAL REFLECTION:
List 3 things which you are worried about today. Why are you worried?

_____

_____

_____

How does worry usually affect you? Physically? Emotionally? Spiritually? How can you see your life improving in these areas as you turn your worries over to God?

_____

_____

_____

_____

How can a person be aware of their circumstance and the challenges they face without being worried? Where does my faith in God come in?

_____

_____

_____

Who am I praying for?

_____

_____

_____

What am I praying about?

_____

_____

_____

_____

PRAYER STARTER:

Faithful Father, I'm thankful that I do not have to worry about anything so long as I put my trust in You. I walk in confidence today, knowing that You supply my needs and protect me from harm. I appreciate Your care for me and I ask Your forgiveness for the times that I have doubted You. Help me today...

– Amen

Day 3

Credit Check

*"For what saith the scripture? Abraham believed God
and it was counted unto him for righteousness."*
Romans 4:3

May I ask you a personal question? Do you know your credit score?
I ask because, let's face it – nowadays having good credit is just
as important as having a savings account. Sometimes even more.
Having cash with bad credit will still get you hassled. Unless you
can pay in full, you may have to spend more of your hard-earned
money even if you have cash on hand. Unfortunately, that's the
world in which we live. You can have good credit and little cash
on hand, and you can still get pretty far. Good credit can take
you places. Trust me, I've heard. Bad credit is no fun. Trust me,
I know.

Recently I've made the decision to become financially secure.
That means research, investments, discipline, saving money,
paying off bills, creating a budget... all the tools necessary in
order to get my financial life together. It's been a struggle, but I've
been motivated to stay the course. Mostly because I've discovered
what credit means. Good credit means you are trustworthy. You
are responsible. You aren't a flake. You aren't wishy washy. You
are a person of your word. You don't overextend yourself. You
don't spend beyond your means. Good credit means that you can
be counted on to come through.

So why do we need credit anyway? Sometimes necessary
purchases must be made and you don't have the cash on hand
to make them. Take a house, for example. If you're planning on

striking out on your own, you're going to need a roof over your head. However, most of us will never have an extra $400,000 laying around. (If you do, please call me. I need to talk to you. NOW!) That's where credit comes in. Simply put, credit helps us get what we need before we can afford it. Now let's take another look at Abraham.

When the Bible mentions God and HIS credit, you can be absolutely sure that I'm going to pay attention. You should too. After all, I'd at least like to see what kind of credit score God has. Don't you? Aren't you even just a little bit curious as to what kind of home or car God can afford according to Equifax, Transunion and Experian. The Bible says, "The cattle upon a thousand hills" belongs to God but I would still like to see if the Almighty could be approved for a home equity loan. Don't you?

As it turns out, God's credit covers more than the material. It goes to the heart of what His children really need. More than anything else, we need to be saved. We need fresh starts. We need new opportunities. That's exactly what Abraham couldn't afford on his own. We can't either. However, that's exactly what Jesus paid for with His sacrifice and gives us by His blood. We couldn't afford it, so God makes us righteous in Him. "Abraham believed God and it was credited to him as righteousness". Abraham was covered by the blood of Jesus and viewed as if he had never sinned. Why? How come? It's because of God's credit. God basically gave Abraham righteousness on credit, simply because Abraham believed what God had to say. Abraham went from having no righteousness in hand to having the righteousness of God, simply because God extended Abraham a line of credit that Abraham could have never otherwise afforded. Come to think of it, that's the only way Abraham could have obtained God's righteousness. He couldn't pay for it. Would never deserve it. It had to be extended as a gift BEFORE we could ever earn the right to have it. It had to be given to Abraham on credit. That's the way we receive it too. This is the essence of righteousness by faith. It's the idea that God graciously saves us because we could never afford to save ourselves. What we can afford to do is believe that God performs this miracle in our lives. We may not always be able to trace it and we may not see growth manifested every day, but God is working. God is there. Every day that you walk with Jesus He is working on you and working in you to make you more like Him. Our job is to believe it. Our job is to receive it. Our job is to accept the line of credit that is being offered to us today. I could never afford it on my own, God gives it to me anyway, and that is credit I am extremely thankful for.

PERSONAL REFLECTION:
How can God see us as righteous even when our lives say otherwise?

_____

_____

_____

_____

What is the difference between accepting God's righteousness and assuming that God ignores our flaws? Why should that difference matter?

_____

_____

_____

_____

Can you explain righteousness by faith in one sentence 10 words or less? Write that sentence below. How does the sentence you have written deepen your faith in God?

_____

_____

_____

_____

Who am I praying for?

_____

_____

_____

_____

What am I praying about?

_____

_____

_____

_____

PRAYER STARTER:

Faithful Father, thank You for counting me righteous in You. I accept the credit You have extended towards me and I praise You for the sacrifice of Your Son, Jesus, that makes my new life possible. Please forgive those times that I have taken Your forgiveness for granted. Help me today...

– Amen

Day 4

Baggage Check

"Therefore they inquired further of the Lord, "Has the man come here yet?" So the Lord said "Behold, he is hiding himself by the baggage." I Samuel 10: 22 (NASB)

I tend to overpack, and because I travel quite a bit this is a habit that I definitely need to overcome. I've been known to have a carry-on, and a personal item, and a piece of checked luggage – all for a weekend trip. I can't say this is something that I'm proud of, but I am willing to admit that this is something I habitually do. It's a problem, especially because the more baggage you carry, the more costly the trip. It pays to travel light. It's always in the traveler's best interest to get rid of as much baggage as possible, and if you can help it, to barely carry any at all.

In my defense however, I will say this… It's hard to leave home without your stuff. You and I both have had that sinking feeling in the pit of our stomachs that comes from having left home forgetting the stuff you really need. There's nothing as disappointing as opening your suitcase and realizing that your undergarments aren't there (That was a rough weekend, for sure). It's heartbreaking to have to purchase something again that you know you already have when you could have just as easily packed it and taken it with you. So out of fear we overpack. I can't say that I blame you. You probably don't blame me. However, the fact remains that in an effort to protect ourselves against an uncertain future, we end up carrying around a whole lot of stuff we could have left behind.

What is luggage anyway? At its very least, luggage is the stuff we have at home that we've insisted on carrying with us. That stuff is a part of our past. That stuff is a part of our comfort zone. That stuff is a part of our identity. Open our luggage in an airport and the owner should be able to identify his or her baggage by the stuff inside, even if the outside of their bag looks identical to someone else's. In a sense, our luggage is a sampling of who we are, and we hold on to it for dear life. Lose our luggage and we are upset. Destroy our luggage and we feel the loss. That's our stuff in there! For many, the past is precious, even if the possibility exists of a future that can yield so much better and give us so much more.

Saul was ready for his new assignment, or so he thought. As the newly appointed first king of Israel, Saul was to be set aside for his new duties in front of the entire nation by the prophet Samuel. The coronation promised to be more spectacular than anything Israel had ever seen before. For the first time in history the sons and daughters of former Egyptian slaves would crown a monarch that would stand as the head of their government and represent them as they took their place in the world. By all accounts, the Lord had chosen the right man for the job. Handsome and intelligent, with an imposing stature and commanding presence, God handpicked the tallest man in the kingdom. Saul looked like a king, Saul walked like a king, and by the end of the day Saul would be the undisputed king of the nation of Israel. There was only one problem... Saul did not show up.

The officiants assembled, and the crowds began to gather from the four corners of the kingdom, but there was no king to be crowned. Saul was nowhere to be found. "Maybe he's running late?" They wait until the wait became uncomfortable and the people began to ask questions. Finally, having received no answers from each other, they decided to ask the Lord. God knew exactly where Saul was. God was very familiar with Saul's hiding place. Like a father chasing toddlers in a game of hide-and-seek, God has seen that exact hiding spot time and time again. Frightened by the brightness of his future, Saul chose to hide in the shadows of his past. The Bible says he had hidden himself "among the baggage".

Saul ran away from his future assignment and hid among the comfortable stuff he carried with him from home. It wasn't anything he needed, to be sure. His former life had little to do with where God was taking him. If he was honest with himself, nothing from his past was going to be relevant to his future. A king would require new clothes, new tools, and even a scepter and a crown. I doubt he had anything resembling a scepter or a crown tucked away in his baggage. He didn't really need the baggage anyway, except that it served to be a convenient hiding place. That's exactly where God found him, behind his baggage. That's exactly what God found Saul doing, hiding. That's often where God finds us too.

Far too often God finds us hiding behind our past, refusing to let it go. It may not be pretty, but it's comfortable and it's ours, so we hold on to it for dear life. It's not my place to judge you, but it is my job to remind you- you have a coronation to attend. Your own! God has selected you for greatness, Queen! God has anointed you for a purpose, King! Don't let the stuff from your past hold you back. Travel light. Let it go. The mistakes of your past aren't relevant to where you're headed. Take the message and leave the mess behind. Step into the future God has for you. Don't let your baggage hold you back.

PERSONAL REFLECTION:
Have you identified any challenges from your past that prevent you from fully enjoying your present relationship with God? If so, how do you intend to move forward?

_____

_____

_____

What areas of dysfunction have become comfortable for you? How do you intend to address them?

_____

_____

_____

Have you considered the help of a professional to help you let go of your past? Why or why not? If you have considered it, but not actively sought the help, what has prevented you from taking the next step?

_____

_____

_____

_____

Who am I praying for?

_____

_____

_____

What am I praying about?

_____

_____

_____

PRAYER STARTER:
Faithful Father, thank You for being a God who governs my past, my present and my future. You hold them all in the palm of Your hand and I can trust You with them because of Your love for me. I turn my baggage over to You, and I refuse to allow the mistakes of my past to keep me from living the life You desire and have designed for me. I pray today...

– Amen

Day 5

Another Level

"But if not, be it known until thee, O king, that we will not serve thy gods, nor worship the golden image which thou hast set up." Daniel 3:18

There are levels to just about everything, and that includes your faith. When faced with a fiery execution, the "Three Hebrew Boys" met the test of their faith with the testimony of what God had done for them. Based on what God had done for them and where God had brought them from they could claim beyond the shadow of a doubt that "God is able". It was God's ability that motivated them. It was God's ability that inspired them. It was God's ability that emboldened them. In the presence of a powerful king these young men truly believed that they served an all-powerful God. Theirs was the God who parted the waters of the Red Sea and allowed His children to walk across on dry land. Theirs was the God who sent ten plagues that brought the Egyptians to their knees and brought Pharaoh to an acknowledgement of the greatness of Jehovah. Theirs was the God who knocked down the walls of Jericho and handed the city over to His people- conquering that kingdom without much of a fight. They had seen their God work miracles time and time again. So, when these men spoke they were not guessing, they were not stalling, and they weren't making anything up. Shadrach, Meshach and Abednego meant every word that they said when they declared that "God is able". They declared that God was able because He had repeatedly proven that He was.

That's one level of faith. As it turns out, the challenge these young men were about to face required another. What they were up against required more than just an acknowledgment of God's ability. What they were up against required a whole lot more.

I grew up with a song by legendary gospel artist Andre Crouch entitled "Through It All". The song begins:

> *"I've had many tears and sorrows,*
> *I've had questions for tomorrow,*
> *there's been times I didn't know right from wrong,*
> *But in every situation,*
> *God gave me blessed consolation,*
> *that my trials come to only make me strong"*

Like most people who heard it, I loved that song! The encouraging message of trials that are used as a canvas upon which God can paint a portrait of His glory was enough to inspire anyone who heard the music, to hold on. It was the second verse, however, that really got my attention:

> *"I thank God for the mountains,*
> *and I thank Him for the valleys,*
> *I thank Him for the storms He brought me through,*
> *For if I'd never had a problem,*
> *I wouldn't know God could solve them,*
> *I'd never know what faith in God could do."*

That was the line that really stuck with me. The last phrase, in particular, was the phrase that really inspired me. "I'd never know what faith in God could do." It was as if Andre was talking to everyone who had ever experienced challenging times and encouraging them to hang on, because the obstacles they faced, big or small, were really opportunities for God to "show up and show out." I heard that song, and that line, and it helped to fashion for me an idea of what faith really is. To me faith became more than recognition that a powerful God exists, but a connection with that God and a belief in what He could DO. He could DO the impossible. He could DO whatever I needed. He wasn't hindered or hampered by anything. That was the basis of my faith.

That was a good start, but as I would soon find out, I still had farther to go. After all, there are levels to just about everything, and that includes our faith.

I think I started where the Hebrew boys once began... where everybody begins. We all begin by believing in what God can do. God's resume is impeccable. God's ability is irrefutable. He created the universe after all! You can't argue with that! So, we believe in God because of what He can do, and then one day things change. Something happens, and God doesn't do what we want, or even what we think we need. This is where faith is commanded to grow. This is where the stakes are raised. This is where life ups the ante, and our faith is taken to another level. This is where we stop believing in what God can do and start trusting God because of who He is.

The Hebrew boys respond to Nebuchadnezzar the only way they knew how. Based on their experiences, they were able to refute his claim. The king had implied that God was not able and that simply was not true- God is able! God could recuse them if He chose to and His rescue would be welcomed, and amazing. Not only was what the king claimed simply not true, but what the king claimed simply did not matter. Their faith had gone beyond the elementary. Their faith had grown past the ordinary. Even if God chose not to rescue them, they would not betray their trust in Him. That's the kind of faith that's been taken to another level.

Faith should begin with God's ability (God is able). There can be no authentic faith without an acknowledgement and some understanding of the ability of God. God IS able. God can do anything! Faith starts there, but eventually faith needs to grow, mature, and even graduate and move out into the challenging world. Faith in God's ability must develop and mature into faith that is loyalty. We must grow out of "God is able" and grow into "But if not". God has done so much for me, but He is so much to me and THAT is why I trust Him. I trust God because I love Him. I depend on God because we are in a relationship. I serve God because He is my Father and I am His child. This is the kind of faith that has graduated and grown. That is faith that has gone to another level.

PERSONAL REFLECTION:
Name three things that God has done for you over the past 12 months that have increased your faith in Him:

_____

_____

_____

_____

What are the dangers of basing faith on what God has done for us and not on our loyalty to God?

_____

_____

_____

_____

When was the last time God refused to grant your request and you trusted anyway? What did that experience teach you about faith in God?

_____

_____

_____

_____

Who am I praying for?

_____

_____

_____

_____

What am I praying about?

_____

_____

_____

_____

PRAYER STARTER:

Faithful Father, I thank You for all that You have done and all that You are doing in my life. I am grateful for the miracles that have taken place, the prayers You have answered, and the dreams that have come true. While I am thankful for the times You have said "yes", I am also grateful for the times You have said "no" and spared me from trouble I could not see. Forgive me for the times when I was not loyal and did not place my trust in You. Help me today...

– Amen

Day 6

He Knows

"Declaring the end from the beginning, and from ancient times the things that are not yet done, saying, My counsel shall stand, and I will do all my pleasure."
Isaiah 46:10

What are your plans for today? If you're like me, you've already made them. Your calendar was set last night and the notifications started buzzing early this morning. It's time to go! There are deadlines to be met, there are tasks to be completed, there is stuff to be done! We are all busy people who lead busy lives (I'm surprised that you have time to read this devotional. Kudos to you!) Whatever your plans are, I'm sure you are working your hardest and doing your best. We all have our plans, but there's something about those plans that you may or may not have considered... There's no way of ensuring that your plans come to pass.

History and experience have taught us this painful lesson time and time again. Ask the unsuspecting victims of the Enron scandal about security and they'll tell you that it doesn't exist. Not really. Not when executives you've never met can make bad decisions of which you were not apart which causes you to lose a pension you were depending on in order to retire with dignity. Ask the victims of the most devastating terror attack on American soil to-date about security and they'll tell you that it can be compromised by religious fanatics who have decided to fly planes into buildings- using the most unsuspecting methods imaginable in an effort to bring the most powerful nation on earth to its knees. Ask the victims of hurricane Katrina, or any natural disaster that has destroyed property and devastated lives about security, and the survivors will tell you that nature has a way of showing up unannounced and uninvited and turning every plan that you've created on its head, leaving you distressed and disconsolate in the wake of the disaster. Security is what you make it, unless life decides to make it something else entirely.

Our plans are not as certain as we think they are. We'd like to think that we are prepared, insulated and secure, the truth of the matter is that we are subject to the whims of circumstance and the will of God. Plans are never really set in stone. Truth be told, the best we can do is hope for the best. We make plans for the weekend, but we aren't sure if we'll live to see the weekend get here. We make plans to travel, but we aren't sure if finances will allow us the privilege. We save for retirement, but we aren't sure that an unforeseen crisis will not wipe out our nest egg altogether. I don't know about you, but all this uncertainty doesn't do anything to lessen my stress levels or help with my anxiety. It probably doesn't do much for you either. Read the last paragraph again and this time, notice how you feel. If you're like me, you feel insecure. You feel uncertain. You feel a little bit scared.

I'd be more confident and more comfortable if I knew what was up ahead. If I had the plan in front of me, I'd feel better about it. Honestly, I don't even need to edit it or approve it, but it would be nice to see it. It would be nice to know what was waiting for me beyond tomorrow. It would be nice to know where the potholes are, so I could avoid them. It would be nice to know where the pitfalls are, so I could prepare for them. What bothers me even more than life's uncertainty is my inability. My inability to see. My inability to plan. My inability to know.

There is no way of knowing. You've tried. I've tried. Nothing works. We try to know the weather before it happens, and we end up soaked in rain after receiving forecasts of sunny days.

We try to predict the behaviors of others only to look into the cameras after the latest tragedy and tell the world that we had no idea what our friends, neighbors and even our children were capable of. We claim, with tears in our eyes, that there was no way of knowing what anger was brewing inside. We try to use every tool available to predict our circumstances and control our environment, but we're caught off guard over and over and over again. As difficult as it may be to admit, when it comes to what lies ahead, there is no way of knowing. We just don't know.

Speaking of knowing, do we really want to? If you knew the day of your death, would it give you any comfort or would you be so preoccupied with dying that you would forget to live? If you knew what tragedy waited for you just around the corner, would you stay indoors afraid to get out of bed or would you move forward boldly accepting the future as it unfolded? Chances are, even if we knew the challenges that awaited us, we wouldn't be able to do anything about them anyway. We wouldn't be able to avoid them. We wouldn't be able to stop them. We would only be tormented by a knowledge that we would be completely unable to handle. When it comes to the future, not only are we unable to know, but prudence suggests that we may not want to know.

Thankfully, faith has determined that we don't have to know. We can wake up tomorrow having planned and prayed with absolutely no idea how things will turn out. With every confidence that the God who knows the end from the beginning has already provided for every need and waits on the other side of the sunrise to help with every problem that comes our way. We can be encouraged because God knows! He knows our past and loves us anyway, He knows where we are right now and refuses to give up on us. He knows what tomorrow holds and invites us to trust Him because He holds tomorrow. God knows, and because He knows, we can simply trust in Him.

I'm grateful for the security I have because I planned. I'm even more thankful for the faith I have in God because at the end of the day, He knows.

PERSONAL REFLECTION:
How should the fact that God knows everything about you affect your relationship with Him? Should anything change about the way that you pray? Trust? Serve?

_____

_____

_____

Is there anything God knows about you that makes you uncomfortable? Is there any detail about your life that you hesitate to bring before God in prayer?

_____

_____

_____

_____

Are you comfortable with the fact that God knows the future and yet does not prevent pain? Why or why not?

_____

_____

_____

_____

Who am I praying for?

_____

_____

_____

What am I praying about?

_____

_____

_____

_____

PRAYER STARTER:

Faithful Father, I praise You as the Omniscient One! You know everything about me and yet You still love me. You know everything that will ever happen to me and You have pledged to bring me through. I thank You for always watching over me and I trust You with my yesterdays and my tomorrows. I pray today that...

– Amen

Day 7

Do More Than Just Believe

"Thou believest that there is one God; thou doest well: the devils also believe, and tremble." James 2:19

I don't "believe". Not anymore. Man does THAT sound weird to say. I mean, how can you possibly write a book about faith if, in fact, you don't believe! Isn't that the prerequisite to talking about faith? Isn't that the foundation of being a Christian? If nothing else, don't we at least have to believe? I can hear the questions off in the distance. I can read the comments about how I've lost my marbles coming a mile away. I can feel your concern through these pages. You're worried about me. Don't be. You're probably talking about me. Make sure you recommend this book. Some of you are even praying for me. I appreciate it. I'm fine. I promise. It's just that, personally, I've come to a point where I can no longer just...believe.

Confused? Well Maybe I should clarify. Give me a moment to explain: Belief is a part of entry-level, basic Christianity. The Bible also teaches that belief is the foundation of faith. We got that honestly... "He that cometh to God must believe that He is..." (Hebrews 11:6).

Think of belief as "Faith 101". My problem with belief, however, is that so many of us – too many of us, get stuck right there. The Bible has something else to say about belief... it's common. It's not special at all. You believe? Good for you, but just know that anyone can do it. It doesn't take anything extra special to believe. According to the Bible, "The devils believe and tremble."

Honestly, that's the problem. That's what challenged

me. That's what troubled me. That's what changed me. That statement is the reason why I no longer "believe." Question: If on my Christian journey, God is calling me to new and higher heights of growth with Him every day, should I have more and deeper faith than the demons do? If they have managed to believe, shouldn't I do more than just believe? Come to think of it, of course the demons believe! Why shouldn't they? They have seen God's power first hand. They know that God works miracles. They have seen God's people delivered time and time again. They've been on the losing end of too many battles not to know that God can provide for and protect His people. Of course, the demons believe! They have the experience. They've seen the evidence. Belief is good enough for them, but it should in no way be good enough for you and me.

God's enemies may have evidence and experience with God's power, and it stands to reason that they have even felt His presence. When they are losing another battle as God defends His children, they know that the "Lord of hosts" has shown up once again. God's opponents may have evidence and experience, but one thing they do lack is a relationship. If they acknowledge God, it's not from a heart of love. If they do God's will, it's not because they are grateful for His grace. They just don't have the relationship with God that God's children do. His works aren't special to them. His grace doesn't move them. For those who claim to follow Jesus and walk by faith, however, things should be different. We call ourselves believers, and there's nothing wrong with the title. We should be, however, so much more. For us, Jesus is more than just a statement of fact. For us God is more than just the conclusion of a well-crafted apologetic argument used to prove His existence and justify our religious affiliations. For us God is a father. For us God is a friend. For us God is a provider. For us God is a healer. We don't just recognize God, we have a relationship with God. We do more than just believe.

So many are stuck in what I like to call "the realm of recognition". Ask 10 people if God exists and the majority will probably tell you yes. They believe in a Higher Power. They believe in some sort of Supreme Being. Somebody created all of this, after all. There's someone out there that set the sun, moon and stars in space and that being is more than likely responsible for our existence. They will tell you that He's known to many different people by many different names. Some will even go so far as to say that He is aware and even active in the affairs of human beings. My assignment here is not to discourage anyone from believing. Rather, I want to challenge you to do more. I want to call you from recognition to relationship. I want to challenge you to do more than know about God, I want to invite you to get to know God. I want to implore you to do more than recognize the fact that He loved the world and invite you to enter into a love relationship with Him. This is what He craves. This is what He desires. This is what we need. This is the goal towards which we must all strive. God wants more than just servants, God wants us to be His friends. He wants us to live in the joy of being His children. He wants us to walk in the security of leaning on His everlasting arms. He wants us to do more than just occasionally acknowledge His name, or recognize His existence. We must do more than just believe.

PERSONAL REFLECTION:
In what ways is belief in God no longer enough for your faith experience? Why do you need more?

_____

_____

_____

_____

How do you understand the differences between belief and faith? How can the two concepts be confused?

_____

_____

_____

_____

In what ways are you determined to "Do more than just believe?"

_____

_____

_____

_____

Who am I praying for?

_____

_____

_____

_____

What am I praying about?

_____

_____

_____

_____

PRAYER STARTER:

Faithful Father, thank You for developing my faith. I want to move past belief in You and begin living the life You have for me. Thank You for leading me on this journey. Forgive me for merely acknowledging Your existence and help me move forward in Your power. Help me today...

– Amen

Day 8

Misplaced Faith

"But Peter declared, "Even if I have to die with you,
I will never disown you." And all the other disciples said
the same." Matthew 27:35

I'm terribly afraid of heights. Which is why I was just as surprised as anyone else when I found myself at the local indoor rock-climbing gym. Trying something new is one thing, but this was something else altogether. Did I mention that I was afraid of heights? Deathly afraid of heights? Yet here I was, strapped into a harness, climbing some 30 feet into the air, trying desperately to convince myself that I was not going to plummet to my death and that everything, in fact, would turn out ok. With every inch I climbed I was reminded of the many times I told myself that I'd never do something like this. I laughed when friends suggested it. I laughed at others who did it. Now here I was, doing the very thing I always promised myself I would never do. I was climbing… and I made it! I made it all the way to the top and back down again in one piece. Nothing cracked except the glass ceiling of limitation I had hanging over my head. I did the very thing I always said I'd never do.

Oh well. Never say never.

I've lived long enough to learn that absolutes should be used with an abundance of caution. Everybody has a laundry list of things they said they'd never do, places they said they'd never go, words they promised they would never say. Everybody has a list, most of us have lived long enough to call the list a liar. Life will humble you by teaching you that the absolutes are outside of your control and the things that are negotiable are more than we realize. The best we can do is talk about the things we hope we would never do. We can plan and prepare and hope and pray, but given the right circumstances, just about anything is possible. Even that which we thought was impossible.

Apparently, Peter didn't get that memo.

Peter is so confident in his relationship with his Lord that he informs Jesus of just how strong the relationship is. "Even if I have to die with you, I will never disown you". Notice Peter's boldness. He doesn't say "I can't see myself disowning you." He says "never". No chance. The possibility doesn't exist. Not gonna happen. And we all know what happens next... Not even 24 hours passes before Peter is choking on his words and choking back the tears of regret. Not even 24 hours has passed, and Peter has done the very thing He told Jesus he would never do. That had to be disheartening. That had to be embarrassing. We would know, we've all been there. Like Peter, we've all done something we said we'd never do. Like Peter, we have all suffered from a case of overconfidence, or rather, a case of misplaced faith.

Where you place your faith is important. By now, most of us are aware that we can't blindly place our faith in others. Experience is a pretty good teacher and experience has done a great job teaching most of us that blind trust is a bad idea. Even after verification, blind trust still isn't always warranted, as people have been known to conceal their intentions and change their minds. If you're looking for a safe place to rest your faith, I wouldn't suggest people. That usually doesn't work out very well.

We're leery of placing our faith in people, but we have been known to place faith in ourselves, and that can be a problem too. Not to be confused with arrogance, self-confidence can be a great thing! Confidence in yourself tends to have a calming effect on those who are around you, especially if you're trying to lead them. I personally find it comforting to know that YOU know that you know what you're doing! Confidence is an attractive quality because people are drawn to those who are sure about who they are and where they are going. Confident people are awesome to be around, and I believe the world needs more of them. The world needs more people who aren't starved for attention or thirsting for affirmation. The world needs more people who aren't afraid to march to the beat of a different drummer or turn their backs to the proverbial crowd. I believe that the world needs more confident people. I also believe that the world needs fewer people who place ultimate confidence in themselves. Believe me, there is a difference.

It's one thing to be unafraid to stand apart, it's quite another to insist that you have to walk alone. It can be downright disastrous to believe that there's no one who can teach you anything, no one who can help you with anything, and no one upon whom you can depend. Of all the people who you think you can trust, you may be tempted to think that you are the most trustworthy. Of all the people in whom you should have confidence, you may be tempted to think you are the most qualified. If anyone is going to fail you, it certainly won't be you. You can pull it off when all else fails. You can make it happen when everyone else deserts you. If you can't believe in anyone else, you certainly can believe in you. I'm begging you... think again.

Peter learned about misplaced faith the hard way. He was 100% sure that He would never ever deny his Lord. He was also 100% wrong. The truth was, he had no idea what he was capable of- none of us do. "The heart is deceitful above all things, and desperately wicked: who can know it?" (Jeremiah 17:9 KJV) The answer to Jeremiah's question is "No one. Not even you." While confidence is desired, misplaced faith can be disastrous. We have limitations that can't be extended. We have flaws that can't be ignored. We have a multitude of reasons and countless examples of why we can't trust ourselves…

And we have a multitude of reasons and even more examples of why we ultimately place our faith in God.

PERSONAL REFLECTION:
Why is it dangerous to be confident in our own spiritual strength?

_____

_____

_____

_____

Since we place our faith in God, how do we acknowledge the gifts God has placed within us?

_____

_____

_____

_____

When was the last time you placed confidence in yourself instead of faith in God and failed? What did you learn from your mistake?

_____

_____

_____

_____

Who am I praying for?

_____

_____

_____

_____

What am I praying about?

_____

_____

_____

_____

PRAYER STARTER:

Faithful Father, I am grateful that when I place my confidence in You, it is never a mistake. I can trust You with every aspect of my life, knowing that You will always do what is best for me. Today I ask You…

_____

_____

_____

_____

_____

_____

_____

_____

_____

_____

_____

_____

_____

_____

_____

_____

_____

_____

_____

_____

– Amen

Day 9

Dealing with Disappointment

"But we trusted that it had been he which should have redeemed Israel: and beside all this, to day is the third day since these things were done." Luke 24:21

Have you ever been disappointed in Jesus? I've been there. I've been there more times than I feel comfortable admitting. I've been there more times than you could possibly know.

Where do I even start? Do I start with the prayers I've prayed as sincerely as I knew how, that felt like they never got past the ceiling- if they even got that high? Or do I start with the times I trusted Jesus to come through only to discover that He and I were on different pages and had different ideas on what "coming through" actually looked like and what "victory" actually was? How about the times when I felt let down and even embarrassed because my best intentions and best prayers weren't enough to produce the answer I desired?

The disappointment hits especially hard when you think about what is happening in your life versus what you and I would have done. I mean, if I had the power God has and I loved me like God says He does, then surely I'd do things differently. I'd DEFINITELY do things differently! No wonder I end up disappointed. The way my expectations are set up shapes what I expect from Jesus. I finally understand Martha! Jesus arrives after Lazarus has died and finds the grieving sister ready for an epic confrontation. "Lord, if you had been here, my brother would not have died." I finally know why she could say that. While Martha is talking to Jesus she's thinking about what SHE would have done. This is Martha, after all she's always where she is supposed to be. She's always doing what she is supposed to do. If SHE had received an urgent request about the illness of one of her closest friends in the world and it was within her power at all to make things better, Martha would have done what Martha was inclined to do. Martha would have fixed it. Martha would have handled it. Martha would have been there. Martha would have come through. Now I understand where you're coming from, Martha. Now I understand.

I've had my fair share of expectations from Jesus. They haven't just materialized out of thin air, to be sure. They're based on who I believe Jesus to be and what I believe Jesus to be able to do. They are based off of my observations of the experiences of others and my interpretations and interactions with the promises I have found in God's Word. I've heard time and time again about the love of Jesus and the power of Jesus and the grace of Jesus and the kindness of Jesus, and I've also been told that He is my friend. I think I understand what it means to be a "friend". I've had my own experiences with friends who were loving, gracious, powerful and kind. Those friends are there for me when I need them. Those friends answer when I call. Their friendship meets my expectations. More often than not, when the chips are down those friends do whatever is within their power to do to make things better. We are friends because we try not to let each other down. Maybe that's why I don't always know what to do about my friendship with Jesus.

My friendship with Jesus poses a problem, because it's not always what I expect a friendship to be. As a matter of fact, sometimes my friendship with Jesus is very different than any other friendship I have. It's different and much more complicated. Meanwhile, Jesus is not trying to win my approval. He doesn't need my permission. He's not afraid to tell me no. He's not afraid of disappointing me. He's not afraid of not doing what I expect Him to do if that is what He thinks is best for my life. How exactly do we deal with someone like that? They can't be manipulated. They can't be controlled. They can't be forced to do anything, and eventually, they will disappoint you. It's bound to happen.

It's not a matter of "if" we will be disappointed, it's a matter of when, and how we choose to deal with the disappointment. There will be times when things do not go our way. There will be requests that are not honored. There will be times when it looks as if you have put all your chips on the table and lost them all because you believed. There will be times when it seems as if Jesus does not meet expectations and does not come through. "But we were hoping He was the One who would redeem Israel".

Can you hear the pain in the voices of Jesus' followers? As they are walking to Emmaus they carry the baggage of disappointment along with them. They laid all their chips on the table. They placed all their trust in One they thought would never fail them. They expected Him to come through. After all, if THEY had started a movement with thousands of followers and people who were looking on the last thing they would have done was die ingloriously for all the enemies and naysayers to see. Of course, they were disappointed, but it's what happens next that gives me hope. They were let down but Jesus never let them go. Jesus jumps right into the middle of their disappointment and helps them to refocus their attention on Him. Their heads are hanging, but Jesus walks beside them. Their steps are dragging, but Jesus travels with them. Jesus is patient with them and teaches them and encourages them.

Jesus never promised that those followers, or any of His followers would avoid the times when He does not meet their expectations. He does promise, however, to never leave us nor forsake us. Have you ever been disappointed in Jesus? Join the club, but never leave His side. Give God another chance. Give

God a little more time. Allow God another opportunity to use life's disappointments to show you exactly who He really is.

PERSONAL REFLECTION:

When was the last time you were disappointed in God? What led to your disappointment? Do you still feel the same way?

_____

_____

_____

_____

List three things you expect God to do for you. Has God always met your expectations? If not, how did that make you feel?

_____

_____

_____

_____

Has God ever done something for you that you were not expecting? If so, write it below and then thank Him for it.

_____

_____

_____

_____

Who am I praying for?

_____

_____

_____

_____

What am I praying about?

_____

_____

_____

_____

PRAYER STARTER:

Faithful Father, I thank You for being a God that exceeds all of my expectations. If You were to simply do what I expected You to do, then You would never bring to fruition the things I did not dare to dream. Thank You for always going above and beyond in my life. Forgive me for trying to imprison You with my expectations. Today I pray…

– Amen

Day 10

Trust the Power

"Accounting that God was able to raise him up, even from the dead; from whence also he received him in a figure." Hebrews 11:19

This was a horrible, horrible plan. Ok. Let's review. After waiting for years for the son he was originally promised, Abraham receives the promised Isaac. Sometime later, Abraham also received a tap on the shoulder with some instructions that seem entirely too incredible to be believed. God Himself commands the father of the faithful to slay his precious son! Isaac is to be sacrificed without explanation or even enough time to say goodbye. There is no line of reasoning to share with Sarah, the boy's mother, because Abraham himself receives no particular reason from God. Nothing comes from the divine except clear directions. "Take now thy son, thine only son Isaac, whom thou lovest, and get thee into the land of Moriah" (Genesis 22:2 KJV). And just when you think things are bad, you realize that they are about to get even worse.

It's one thing for Sarah not to know. Sure, when Isaac didn't come back home Abraham would have had to eventually explain. At least, however, they could have slipped out into the darkness during the early morning hours while Sarah was still asleep. Isaac, however, was awake, alert, and eventually aware of what was happening to him. This wasn't some story being told about which he was the subject. This was a drama in which he was the central participant. There was a sacrifice to be made and without Isaac's consent or foreknowledge, he was involved. He was the sacrifice! He was to be laid on the altar by his 100 plus year old father and expected not to run away or resist. Now I'm really perplexed. Isaac lays himself on the altar and Abraham ties him up, without either of them having any assurances of how this episode would eventually turn out. To be clear: Abraham, based on no other reason other than a command from God, fully intended to kill his son.

I repeat: This was a horrible, horrible plan.

Personally, I wouldn't trust it. I couldn't trust anything about it. There's no way! There's no way I could have stood idly by and just allowed my son to die. Especially after God had promised me this particular blessing. Especially after I've had to wait so long. Especially after I had gone through so much to receive it. Yet, Abraham gets up early in the morning, gathers his stuff along with his son, and sets out on yet another God-led journey. He has heard God's voice before and He has followed God's leading before. He has followed God even when he didn't know where God was taking him. Now Abraham is following God even though Abraham knows exactly what God is asking him to do-and that what God is asking Abraham to do will change everything.

I am most shaken when God asks me to do the uncomfortable, and yet God never stops asking for precisely that. God is constantly asking His children to grow, sacrifice, stretch, and become more and more like Him. We celebrate the growth and yet, we shirk from the harsh reality. We run and hide when confronted with the fact that God will take away things with which you are familiar, God will open doors that are quite uncomfortable to walk through, and God will lead you into places where you sometimes do not want to go- all for your growth and God's glory.

We find it difficult sometimes to trust God's plans because we often do not understand His direction. God is difficult to trace. God cannot be dictated to, or contained, and neither can

God be ignored. At the end of the day God will inevitably get what God wants. God's will is always going to be accomplished. Understandably, we sometimes find it difficult to trust God's plans because we often do not understand His direction. God is difficult to trace. God is nearly impossible to predict. God is definitely in full control, but sometimes His plans seem to be the exact opposite of that. His plans often seem like bad ideas because they take us out of our comfort zones. "God what are you thinking? Do you really expect me to move there? Do you really expect me to do that?" If we had it our way the plans for our lives would always make sense and the numbers would always add up. But let's face it, we've had it all our way before. As a matter of fact, left to ourselves we always have it our way... And it never works out.

The path doesn't always look inviting. The way forward doesn't always seem exciting. However, I must encourage you to follow God. Anyone who has walked with God for any length of time can tell you that His ways are not our ways, but they are always infinitely better. Our plans have no guarantees. God's plans always work out for our good. Our limits get in the way. God is able to make a way. I invite you to trust God even when His plans seem like bad ideas and His purposes seem like they will not come to pass. Trust His plan. Trust His power! The God who can do anything has promised to always come through for you.

PERSONAL REFLECTION:
What is the last thing that God has done in your life that you disagreed with at the time God was doing it? How do you feel about it now?

_____

_____

Abraham was sure that God was the one who gave him the instructions to sacrifice Isaac. How can you be sure when God is talking to you?

_____

_____

_____

What aspects of Christian growth are the most difficult for you? How do you handle them?

_____

_____

_____

Who am I praying for?

_____

_____

_____

What am I praying about?

_____

_____

_____

PRAYER STARTER:

Faithful Father, Your plans don't always make sense to me, but You have never let me down. I praise You for Your faithfulness in my life! Thank You for always being trustworthy even when I do not agree on the paths that You have chosen for me. Please forgive me for the times where I have strayed. Help me today...

– Amen

Day 11

Do You Believe Me?

"And whosoever liveth and believeth in me shall never die. Believest thou this?" John 11:26

We are overwhelmed by so much communication that authenticity is hard to come by. Everybody's always talking about something! On one channel they're trying to sell you something. Some new product that's going to change your life or some new gadget that's going to change the world. Of course, you are the only one that doesn't have it and you are missing out on all the benefits it could bring. But if you act now you can have it for the low price of $19.95 and your life will never be the same. On another channel they are trying to persuade you to do something. The latest data has come out and has definitively proved that the thing you thought was true yesterday is now completely false. This new information is 100% verified and completely foolproof. you should believe them and change now. Your health and happiness depend on it. You can definitely trust them. Why? Well because they are smart and they said so! (Yeah… right).

Facebook runs constant ads. Instagram introduces new products every day. Our emails are swamped with business offers. The mail is flooded with coupons. Google will suggest dozens of new things for you to try and Amazon can now anticipate what you'd like to purchase next. With so many people trying their best to influence your choices, take your money, get some of your time, and invade your private space, it's no wonder why our defenses are up. We just can't let any and everybody into the sanctity of our lives. There just isn't room for everyone and everything! If I purchased every product and joined every gym and tried every diet and watched every movie and believed every talking head that appeared on my television screen, my life would be a confused, convoluted mess. Some things have to get shut out. Some people must be ignored. Some things must go un-experienced and some projects will be left undone. I've got to leave a little on my plate because quite frankly, I'm full. Correction, I'm stuffed! We come across a lot of information every single day. There has to be a limit. There are some things we can't believe.

A healthy skepticism is, well… healthy. It provides protection from the charlatans who would play us for fools. In the midst of society's noise however, our heavenly father reaches out to us. He's also trying to communicate, but with very different motives. He's also trying to connect, but for very different reasons. He wants nothing from you – except your heart. He's not trying to take anything away – except your burdens. He loves you and He cares for you more than anyone ever could.

The airwaves are crowded. It's easy to get overwhelmed and overlook the stuff that's most important. I can see how God would get lost in the shuffle.

Most people will tell you that of all the games they have ever played, the "dating game" is probably the least fun. Whether male or female, just about everyone will agree – dating is hard! (Of course, there is a lot of debate as to which side has it harder, but I'm sure both sides can at least agree on one thing – it's hard!) One of the side effects of dating is that, after a while, a general mistrust can set in. Everyone gets to a point where they've heard it all before. You've heard every promise. You've heard every line. You've seen and heard it all and it's all ended up in the same painful place. It's tough to believe after you've been lied to and hurt. It's tough to listen to the next one who may just be the right one, when you've been listening to the wrong one for so long...

When Jesus stood at the gravesite of one of His best friends Lazarus and talked to a grieving Martha, I'd like to think He knew what He was up against. He knew that He wasn't just sharing empty promises of comfort. He was sharing a powerful resurrection reality that was about to change their lives! One problem: what He was sharing was hard for them to believe. The stuff they saw around them and the reality they lived made believing very difficult. They were bombarded with so much information. A gravesite that told them there was no hope. Mourners that showed them nothing but a future filled with grief. The body of Lazarus had been wrapped and buried. All that information threatened to overwhelm them. Add to that the lies. The lies told by their own grieving hearts and seconded by their superstitions. The lies that had wormed their way into broken hearts and burdened minds. Those lies are dangerous. When you've listened to the wrong message for too long, it becomes hard to believe.

That's why Jesus asked the question: "Do you believe?" Standing in front of them was the opportunity for an amazing miracle, but the question remained "Do you believe"? Jesus was there, standing right in front of them! Anything... everything was possible. The impossible was possible! Not only that, it was promised! But none of that would mean anything, none of that would matter, if they didn't believe.

The promises in the word of God are His expressed will for our lives. These are not the things we have to remind Him to do or convince Him to do, this is what He wants to do for us. Remember, the promises were His idea, not ours. He had plans to bless us before we even knew we wanted to be blessed. God doesn't need His arm twisted. He doesn't need to be convinced. He doesn't need to be prodded or bribed. He will deliver you. He will prosper you. He will come through for you – for no other reason than because He said He would.

And you can always believe what He says.

PERSONAL REFLECTION:
What characteristics of God are most believable to you? How do you deal with the things that you find difficult to believe?

_____

_____

_____

_____

Has there been a time when God has spoken, and you did not believe? What were the consequences of your unbelief?

_____

_____

_____

_____

Write your favorite Bible promise below. What makes this promise so dear to you?

_____

_____

_____

_____

Who am I praying for?

_____

_____

_____

What am I praying about?

_____

_____

_____

_____

PRAYER STARTER:
Faithful Father, I thank You for the promises of Your word. I am grateful that You have always had plans to bless me and have always intended to do what is best for me. Forgive me for not always believing what You have had to say. Help me today…

– Amen

Day 12

Prove It

"No man hath seen God at any time..."
John 1:18a

Warning: You're going to be mad at me. I'm going to get you riled up and you're not going to want to hear it... but hear me out anyway. Ready? Here we go...

You cannot definitively prove the existence of God. That sounds sacrilegious, I'm sure. As a matter of fact, I can already see the steam rising from the top of your head. However, give me a chance to explain. Apologist (those dedicated to defending Christianity through the use of logic and evidence) use their arguments to "defend" God. Theologians use their abilities to explain God. Evangelists use their skill to portray God. Storytellers arrange words in an attempt to describe God. However, even with all of the resources of our intelligence pressed into service, no one has been able to prove the existence of God beyond the shadow of a doubt. Short of having God testify in a court of law I believe it would be impossible to prove His existence – especially to someone who does not choose to believe. The opponents of faith will always find a reason not to accept what the believer holds to be true. Sometimes those opponents will even resort to ridicule and mockery. And they will always have a point. Honestly, there will always be evidence to the contrary. There will always be a reason to doubt and there will always be plenty of doubters. Unfortunately, these things will never change, especially because along with other challenges, God remains unseen.

Wouldn't it be so much easier to prove God's existence if in fact He could be seen? As the old saying goes "seeing is believing", but God has no credible witnesses because no one has ever seen Him! Yes, there are those who claim to have heard from God. Sure, there are a few who have claimed to see God at some point in time, but none of that can be independently verified. The fact remains that there is no indisputable evidence and no way of obtaining any. No test has been created to discover God. No telescope has been built to detect God. No device has ever been created to record God. Even still, we are asked to believe…

That's where faith comes in.

Faith reminds us that the walk of the believer is less about argument and more about experience. Specifically, the believers walk is about individual experience. Each one of us is in an individual relationship with a God that cannot be seen, touched, nor traced, and yet that God is very real. We may not be able to prove Him with the formula, but we can experience Him through our faith.

By faith we experience forgiveness that restores our fractured relationship with Him over and over again. By faith we experience His comfort when life's challenges pull us down. By faith we experience His guidance when we are confused and concerned about what the future holds. By faith we experience and enjoy communion with our Heavenly Father. It is by faith that we know Him. It is through the eyes of faith that we see Him. It is with the heart of faith that we experience Him and that makes our faith the only proof that we will ever need.

PERSONAL REFLECTION:

If you cannot see God, how can you be sure that He is real? List three ways you can be sure below:

_____

_____

_____

Since we are unable to produce physical evidence of the existence of God, what is the best way to share Him with someone who does not believe?

_____

_____

_____

_____

Even though you cannot produce physical evidence, have you taken the time to research the arguments for the existence of God? If so, how much do these arguments help you to believe?

_____

_____

_____

_____

Who am I praying for?

_____

_____

_____

What am I praying about?

_____

_____

_____

_____

PRAYER STARTER:
Faithful Father, I believe that You exist and that You love me. I am honored to have a personal relationship with You and I am comforted by the fact that You hear my prayers and that You guide my every step. Forgive me for the times I have disappointed You. Help me today...

_____

_____

_____

_____

_____

_____

_____

_____

_____

_____

_____

_____

_____

_____

_____

_____

_____

_____

_____

– Amen

Day 13

A Faith Reward

"And he said, Come. And when Peter was come down out of the ship, he walked on the water, to go to Jesus."
Matthew 14:29

"Life is dangerous." That's the phrase that arrested my attention. As I watched a video of frightened people hesitating just before taking leaps of various kinds, I could hear Will Smith's voice in the background. As he explained it, risks in life are unavoidable and death is inevitable. According to Will – enjoying life, a fulfilling, satisfying, abundant life, is the only optional part of the experience. We're all put on earth and allotted a certain amount of time. How we use that time is up to us. I haven't always used my time very wisely. I love the challenge of trying something new. As soon as I finish today's devotional reading, I'm headed to a roller-skating class where I'm sure to be the oldest student (and the one most likely to fall). Then later on this week, I'm going to get some bowling lessons. (I'm a terrible bowler. Nowhere to go but up from here!) I love the challenge of a new experience. I love the feeling of accomplishment that comes with acquiring new skills. I love expanding my knowledge base and making steady deposits into the bank of my brain. However, it wasn't always that way. Growing up I was always a bit of a scaredy cat. I was the kid who would shy away from risk. I was the kid who backed down from the fight. I was the one who ran from the challenge. As brave as I'd like to think I've become, I think there's still some of that scared kid inside of me. Especially when it comes to my faith.

It's tempting to think of faith exclusively in terms of belief. The idea goes something like this: I'm comfortable with the existence of God and I'm pursuing a relationship with God, so I must have faith. After all, "He that cometh to God must believe that He is…" I believe in God, I come to God, so I have faith. Right? Well, not so fast. If you are like me and you kept reading, the rest of the verse challenged you. It made you uncomfortable. That's a good thing. That's exactly what the rest of the verse did for me. The Bible continues… "He that cometh to God must believe that He is and that He is a rewarder…" (Hebrews 11:6) That's the part that got me. Apparently, there's more to faith than believing. Faith is more than a concept. Faith is more than an idea. Faith is more than a notion. Faith goes beyond standing on the edge of life's challenges debating on whether to jump into God's will for you. Faith requires not only that I believe, but I must believe that He is a "rewarder"…

I got my first "official" job at around 14 years old. I was home for the summer and decided that I was completely over being penniless and ready to do something about it. The work was difficult, and the environment left much to be desired. Burger King made sure I wasn't lazy, that's for sure. Burger King also made sure that I got paid every two weeks. I connected the dots and realized that if I made the effort, I would be rewarded. I was hooked! I've been working ever since. Had I simply believed that money was out there in the universe somewhere and passively waited around for an income to suddenly appear, I wouldn't have been rewarded with anything. I couldn't avoid the risk. I couldn't afford staying stuck and standing still. I couldn't afford to stay put. Not if I wanted to see something happen. Not if I wanted to see a reward. That's not how life works. That's not how faith works either.

Most of us claim to have faith but never exercise it. We stand on the edge of life's possibilities hesitant about moving forward, unable to go back. We stay still. We stay stuck. We stay right where we are. Fear holds us prisoner while faith holds the keys to freedom and offers them to us for our use. I can't challenge the fact that you have faith, but I can encourage you to use it. Life is dangerous! Like the disciples in the boat with Peter that night, most of us are simply too preoccupied with life's storms to even think about stepping out of the boat and trying something new. Like Peter discovered in the boat with those disciples, the fact that you've decided to step out and follow Jesus doesn't make the storm go away. The storms won't cease. Challenges will never go away. Life will never get safer, but Jesus could never be more present and able and willing to help. He invites you to come! He wants you to jump! Don't stay stuck in the middle. Don't stay tethered to the edge. Step out. Take the leap. Make the move. Exercise your faith.

It's only when you realize that God is a rewarder that we begin to move towards our reward of a new and deeper experience with Him! It is then that we come to understand that our faith can make us free. We don't have to be stuck or stagnant or sedentary or even still. We can move forward. We can improve. We can progress. We can grow.

God is a rewarder. Step out of your doubts, step forward in faith, and receive your reward today.

PERSONAL REFLECTION:

What are some areas where you waste your time? Starting today, how can you make better use of your time so that you live the life God intends for you?

_____

_____

_____

What risk do you think God is calling you to take in your life? What would happen if you failed? What is stopping you from taking the risk now?

_____

_____

_____

_____

Write down three things you have always wanted to accomplish but never did. What part has fear played in your hesitation? How does faith in God help you conquer fear and move forward?

_____

_____

_____

Who am I praying for?

_____

_____

_____

What am I praying about?

_____

_____

_____

PRAYER STARTER:

Faithful Father, thank You for helping me to conquer my fears! I am confident that as I step out of my comfort zone today that You will be with me and guide me every step of the way. Forgive me for not trusting You to work miracles in my life. Forgive me for limiting Your power. Help me today...

– Amen

Day 14

He'll Get You Home

"Looking unto Jesus the author and finisher of our faith; who for the joy that was set before him endured the cross, despising the shame, and is set down at the right hand of the throne of God." Hebrews 12:2

My mother was many things. A good driver was not one of them. At about 5' 3 1/2" tall (she argued passionately and incessantly for that half inch), she could barely see over the steering wheel. Yet somehow, she always managed to find herself behind the wheel of the largest car she could afford. Whether it was a Cadillac, Crown Victoria or a huge 1976 Chevrolet Impala, mom was all too eager to hit the road. In my humble opinion however, her driving left much to be desired.

Maybe one of the reasons my mother's driving was less than ideal (besides her diminutive stature) was that she basically taught herself how to drive. My mother didn't have a driver's license until I was around 15 years old. Before then? Well, our family purchased a car for $500 and mom just... started driving! My younger brother would yell "Brake" every time my mom approached a stop sign. We'd encourage her to stay in her lane as she drove around the streets of Hillsborough county. And me? I'd sit back feeling just a tad frightened, secretly wondering if we were going to make it home.

The feeling, and the question that came along with it, never really left over the years. Mom's driving didn't change much either. There were close calls and near misses. Once or twice I even thought I saw my life flash before my eyes. It wasn't always easy. The ride wasn't always comfortable. However, I've got to give credit where credit is due. After all of those hair-raising rides I have to admit- mom always got us home. No matter the distance, no matter the traffic, no matter the road conditions, no matter the weather, no matter the detour we had to take... We always made it home. Eventually I learned to trust mom's driving, even when I earned the privilege of driving by myself. There's something to be said for a driver who completes every journey she begins. I would have to believe that the driver in question would be worthy of our trust. I might even be inclined to listen to some advice from a driver like that. After all, it's hard to dismiss a driver who always gets you home.

In the book of Hebrews Jesus is described as the "author and finisher of our faith". Another translation describes Him as the "Pioneer and Perfecter "of our faith. As a Christian, I had to admit that this was one of those well-worn church phrases that we often used but rarely understand. What does the writer really mean anyway? One search yielded two definitions for the word "author". One is "originator" and the other is "captain". Just when I began to get comfortable with the one word picture being painted I came across a definition of "finisher" that made me fall in love. The "finisher "of our faith is according to this definition," the one who completes it and brings it home." Not excited yet? Let me see if I can help.

The picture being painted here is that of a journey. Jesus helps us to begin that faith journey by introducing us to Himself. After all, any conscious Christian knows that "we love Him because he first loved us" (1 John 4:19). Any relationship we have with God was really God's idea, not ours. We've never had to go searching for God, because God has always been the one searching for us. We've never had to go and find God, because God was never the one who was lost – we were. Jesus is the originator of our faith experience. Jesus is indeed the Author of our faith.

Jesus, however, is not the watchmaker that we often think Him to be. He doesn't just set things in motion and leave them to run by themselves. He does more than that. He starts, but He also guides. He is the "Author" of our faith which means that He is not only the catalyst, but He is also the Captain. He not only ensures that our faith walk with God begins, but Jesus also takes interest in and responsibility for the day to day progress and stability of our journey. So many Christians experience the ups and downs of life and believe that God's favor and love for them is just as temperamental. In the opinion of many, we are left to our devices and judged by our occasional deeds and misdeeds. We struggle along trying our best to make it from challenge to challenge hoping that each new sunrise will reveal a day that is better and more successful than the last. We forfeit our precious peace all because we fail to understand that God is always near. He never leaves our side, just like He promised. You may feel as if you're journeying alone, and you may even feel as if the burdens you are made to travel with are too much for you to bear. You may be traveling through a storm- but listen! This is your Captain speaking… "Fear thou not; for I am with thee: be not dismayed; for I am thy God" (Isaiah 41:10). He will never leave your side.

The best news about this text is just up ahead. Jesus is the "Finisher" of our faith. Jesus helps us to begin the journey, He guides us along the way, and He finishes what He started. Isn't that good news? That Jesus is a Finisher is good news for everyone who has ever wondered whether or not they could actually make it. It's good news for anyone who has ever worried about surviving. This is good news for anyone who has ever worried about crossing life's finish line. "Am I going to make it? Am I really going to be ok? With all that I've gone through and the mistakes that I've made, can Jesus save someone like me?" The answer is, "Yes Jesus can!" Jesus will see you through! Storms will continue to rage, but God will navigate you through. Obstacles may block your way, but God will guide you through. Jesus is the Beginner, the Sustainer and the Finisher of your faith journey with God, that means that you can trust Him.

He's a good driver after all. He started you out, He will guide you, and He will bring you home.

PERSONAL REFLECTION:
How is your confidence in God increased by knowing that God's promises are His ideas, not ours?

_____

_____

_____

_____

List three non-material ways in which God sustains you daily?

_____

_____

_____

How does it make you feel to know that God has taken responsibility for your Christian growth and maturity as the "Finisher" of your faith?

_____

_____

_____

_____

Who am I praying for?

_____

_____

_____

_____

What am I praying about?

_____

_____

_____

_____

PRAYER STARTER:
Faithful Father, I thank You for loving me enough to desire spiritual growth for me. Please forgive me for the times I have worried about my salvation and did not place my trust in You. Please help me today…

– Amen

Day 15

Incomplete

"And straightway the father of the child cried out, and said with tears, Lord, I believe; help thou mine unbelief."
Mark 9:24

I'm a gold mine of good ideas. They pop into my head just about every other day. Book ideas. Business ideas. Gift ideas. Places I'd like to visit. Things I'd like to do. I even have an idea for a kid's television show starring myself as a superhero (I admit, that one needs some work). The point is: the notepad on my phone is chock-full of plans, proposals and potential. The problem is: most of it never gets done.

When an idea is new, it's exciting. There are all sorts of possibilities. The dream can take any form. The path can lead to any direction. There are no critics, no naysayers, no boundaries, no limits. It's just the creator and the imagination, and the energy that comes from beginning. That energy is intoxicating. That energy is invigorating. That energy... usually dies once reality hits and I ask myself the questions that usually bring me back down to earth and bring my dreams down into their final resting places.

I once heard that "Doubt kills more dreams than failure ever could". If I'm being honest, I've not only heard it- I've lived it. It's not the failure of my projects that aborts them before they are born, it's the doubt. The doubt that I'm qualified enough to be taken seriously. The doubt that I'm skilled enough to actually bring the idea to life (Thanks for that one, Kymone Hinds!). I'm plagued with doubts, as we all are, and it is those doubts that stall the progress. It is doubt that kills most dreams. We often lay the blame of our failures at the feet of external enemies who did not support us or did not believe in us or who somehow blocked our way. We are concerned and even obsessed with the "haters" and the hinderers from without, but I've discovered that what really keeps us stuck and stationary is really the doubt that rises from within.

We doubt because, in some respects, we don't understand. We don't understand how we can accomplish the task set before us. We don't understand the path God has chosen for us. It doesn't make sense. We don't understand. Are these trials really effective teachers? Were these experiences necessary? There's so much we just don't understand:

We don't understand the logistics of God's plan. God's logic is, at the very least… different. He lays out His plans for our lives and they often leave us confounded. Do I really have to do it that way? Must the plan include so many twists and turns? What about these people? These problems? Must it be so difficult? Is all of this critical to the plan?

We don't understand God's purpose of God's plan. Why is God doing this anyway? Studies have shown that people can endure more so long as they understand why. Purpose strengthens us, and not understanding the purpose behind God's plan can make calamity very challenging. When I'm in the middle of a difficult season that is not the time for me to be left with more questions than answers. Go to the book of Job and start reading. You'll find him in chapter 2 sitting in a pile of ashes asking why. You'll also find that he agrees with me. Not knowing the purpose of God's plan can be at best, annoying.

We don't understand the timing of God's plan. Even if we accept the fact that God has a plan and a purpose for the plan, it is still difficult to deal with God's timing. Even if I can wrap my mind around the "what" and the "why", that still leaves the

GAMAL T. ALEXANDER

matter of "when". And what about the "when"? When will it be my turn? When does this stop? When do I win? When can I look forward to progress? How long will I be stuck? How long will I grieve? How long will I hurt? How long will I be lonely? How long will the conflict last? God's timing is not our timing, but when we are in the middle of a struggle it can seem as if God is always late. For a God who operates outside of time, His sense of timing can be hard to understand.

There's so much about how God works and why God works and when God works that is difficult to understand, and our lack of understanding can make it difficult to believe. Therefore, I can sympathize with this father of this hurting child. The child's self-destructive behavior slowly destroyed the father's resolve and he found himself running on empty as he used the last of his patience to get to Jesus. He had already dealt with Jesus' faithless followers who were really no help at all, and now he had reached the end of his rope. There was so much about this he did not understand! Why a child? A child didn't do anything to deserve this. Why so long? The boy had been dealing with this for far too long. Why couldn't the child be healed? Dad had always been taught about a God who could do anything...

There was so much the father could not understand. There was so much that caused the father to doubt. But a good idea was just around the corner. Here it is: he couldn't explain everything, but he didn't have to. He didn't understand everything, but he didn't have to. His was a revolutionary idea: Even if my faith in Jesus is riddled with doubt and incomplete, I can go to Him with what I have. His was a revolutionary request: Help thou mine unbelief.

Jesus heard him, and Jesus helped him, because that is what Jesus does. He wants to help all of us. Jesus placed that boy back into the arms of his father, and I believe Jesus wants us to get past the doubts that keep us from clinging to Him. Your faith may be incomplete, but your God makes up the difference. With the little faith you have, hold on to God today.

PERSONAL REFLECTION:

In what ways do you still struggle to believe? How do you think God feels about your lack of faith?

_____

_____

_____

Now that we understand that we don't need to have the answers to every question in order to follow God, how will that affect how we explain God to others?

_____

_____

_____

_____

Many times, we don't understand God's purpose, God's plan, or God's timing. Are there other things about God that you don't understand? How do they affect your relationship with him?

_____

_____

_____

_____

Who am I praying for?

_____

_____

_____

What am I praying about?

_____

_____

_____

PRAYER STARTER:

Faithful Father, even though I do not understand everything, the things that I do understand still cause me to give You praise! Thank You for revealing Yourself to me day by day and helping me to grasp Your plan for my life. Forgive me for not trusting You more. Help me today...

– Amen

Day 16

Why He Believed

"And he believed in the LORD; and he counted it to him for righteousness." Genesis 15:6

When it comes to having faith, no one is more celebrated than Abraham. When we think about believing God's promises, his is the first name that comes to mind. And for good reason: Abraham BELIEVED God! To Abraham, God's commands were more than intriguing suggestions. For Abraham, God's promises were more than dreams that could one day come true. For Abraham, belief in God was not optional. As far as Abraham was concerned, if God said something, it was good as done. Abraham didn't hedge his bets. Abraham followed. Abraham trusted. Abraham believed! From the time he is introduced to us until the time he is inducted into the "Faith hall of fame", we see Abraham walking by faith. Day by day. Step by step. Over and over again.

The more I think about the strength and intensity of Abraham's faith, the more incredible his faith seems. Consider the following: Abraham's faith journey begins when God taps him on the shoulder and sends him on a trip with absolutely no directions. "Get thee out of thy country, and from thy kindred, and from thy father's house, unto a land that I will shew thee" (Gen 12:1). Abraham's faith walk continues as the "Father of the Faithful" steadily follows God's lead to Egypt, and then into Canaan- never doubting the God that was guiding him. For Abraham the formula was simple. God leads, Abraham follows. God speaks, Abraham listens. God promises, Abraham believes. No wonder we're captured by Abraham's faith. Who wouldn't want to have faith like that! We all do! I want that kind of simple faith! I want the kind of faith that follows God through the good times and bad. I want the kind of faith that holds on to God's promises even though circumstances try to convince me to let go. I want to go when God says go, and go where God says go. For the believer, that's what following God is all about.

Confession: I doubt God way too often. I trust God way too little. For someone who has experienced God in so many ways, It's concerning. As much as I talk faith and sing faith and testify faith, faith is difficult for me to apply. As far as my eyesight goes, every eye test I've taken says I'm nearsighted which for me means I can barely see past the nose on my face. Distance is difficult for me, so I tend to get nervous when I sense that there's something up ahead. I can see the shape but not the details. My physical eyesight is challenging, but my faith is just as bad.

Spiritually speaking, I'm incredibly nearsighted. I can't see past the moment. I can't look into the later on. I can't peep around the corner into tomorrow. Distance is a problem for me and that makes me nervous about the things that are up ahead. I can sense a future coming, but I can't see the details, and that scares me. My nearsightedness makes faith hard for me. Your nearsightedness probably makes faith hard for you as well. We stop trusting God the minute we can no longer trace Him. We stop believing that God will help the minute we can no longer see His hand. We worry. We complain. We cry. We fail. We don't believe. What makes this even more challenging is all the evidence we have to help us to believe! Have you ever thought about all that's available to us today? Many bookstores have entire sections devoted to the subject of faith. There are websites constructed to help increase our faith. We hear sermons weekly that teach us how to have faith. We have the Bible in dozens of versions and it portrays stories of faith. All of this is available. Not to mention movies, music, podcasts, articles, apps, and other resources I don't have space to mention right now. You would think that after all of that, we would have faith! (My oldest daughter's name is Faith!) And yet with all of this, we don't have one of the most essential pieces of the Christian experience. Maybe we're missing something...

We admire Abraham's faith, but are we really seeing it for what it is? Abraham doesn't have a Bible, yet He believes. Abraham doesn't have a church to attend regularly, yet He believes. Abraham doesn't have a devotional journal (although I think he would have really enjoyed this one...), he doesn't have an app or a website or a podcast or a bible study class or any of the things that are available to us to help us build our faith. Abraham hasn't heard a sermon on the radio nor has he watched a service on the Internet- yet Abraham believed God. Ok, now I'm sure that I'm missing something. Fewer materials. Fewer conveniences. Fewer resources. More faith. How? Why?

I took another look at Abraham, and I think I know why He believed. "Now the Lord had said to Abram..." (Gen 12:1). Yep, that's it! "The Lord had said..." Abraham believed God because he had a personal experience with God! When we're introduced to Abraham, we are introduced to a conversation between God and Abraham. They had a talk. Abraham recognized God's voice and responds. No wonder he has faith in God, Abraham knows the God of his faith! Abraham knows God for himself, and when you have a personal experience with God, you can't help but believe.

As I'm writing this, a random thought just came to me: "It's time to update my resume." I'm not looking for another job but hey... my dream job as CEO of Chick-fil-A might be just around the corner. You never know! At its most basic, your resume is a collection of your experiences. It is designed to help build a prospective employer's confidence in your competence and abilities. What does God's resume look like in your life? Is He competent? What about His ability? Your confidence in God will grow when your experiences with God get added to your life's resume. Abraham had an experience of talking with God and hearing from God... that's why he believed.

Why not let God update His resume in your life today?

PERSONAL REFLECTION:

List three reasons why you believe in God? How is your belief strengthened by your experience with God?

_____

_____

_____

How would you explain to someone else what an experience with God is like?

_____

_____

_____

Since experiences are subjective and individual, how can you be certain of their authenticity? What guides your experience with God?

_____

_____

_____

_____

_____

Who am I praying for?

_____

_____

_____

What am I praying about?

_____

_____

_____

PRAYER STARTER:

Faithful Father, I praise You because I have experienced You! I am thankful for the relationship that we share and for testimonies that I have which no one can ever take away. Forgive me for the areas in my life where I do not bring You honor. Help me today...

– Amen

Day 17

It's Up to You

"Then touched he their eyes, saying, According to your faith be it unto you." Matthew 9:29

I've always had an up and down relationship with my car. After all the years we've been together, you'd think that by now the Gold Camry and I would be the best of friends. That isn't always the case. Most of the time we get along great. My car needs something, I come through. My car needs oil, I change the oil. My car needs gas, I fill the tank. No problem. There are rare occasions, however, when my car and I don't really see eye to eye. Sometimes I ignore what my car is trying to tell me. To be honest, I don't always want to be bothered. I don't always want to hear from my precious vehicle. So, every now and then, my car has to teach me a lesson.

One day my car decided to do just that – teach me a lesson I would not forget. I have been driving for quite some time and I had willfully ignored the bright yellow gasoline light that lit up on my dashboard. It was an inconvenient interruption that I just didn't want to deal with at the time. So, I told myself that I had more gas than the car was letting on. It was fine. It has to be! Didn't I just fill up last week? I promised myself, and my car, that before I went anywhere tomorrow I would be sure to fill up the gas tank. I thought my car and I understood each other. I thought everything was fine. So, imagine my surprise as my car eventually slowed down and stalled on the side of the road leaving me stranded. I was surprised, but I was also upset. Ok, I'll admit it. I was MAD! Furious! Enraged! Irate! How could my car do this to me? I was upset at the car and the gas light and the gas tank and everything in the world... until it hit me that at that moment, the only person I really had any right to be upset at was myself. The situation I was in was completely and totally 100% my fault. I had every right to be angry, but the anger should have been directed at the man looking back at me in the mirror. I had made the decision not to fill the car. I had decided to drive by the gas stations. Nobody did that but me. The fact is, cars have not changed much since I got my first one as a Junior in college. If you put gas in them, they will go. The more gas you put in, the further the vehicle will take you. In short, the car you're driving will take you as far as you've prepared it to go. The distance you cover on the journey is all up to you.

While fuel moves our vehicles, faith moves the hand of God. In the text we are studying Jesus performs the miracle "according to your faith". The faith is fueling the miracle! The miracle is traveling as far as the amount of faith available will take it. Think of faith as fuel, and you quickly discover where you and I are missing out. What if the miracles you wanted to receive required the fuel of your faith? What if the all-powerful God acted in proportion to the intensity of your trust in Him? What if God was willing and able to work wonders in your life but was unwilling to work without your belief? What if victory in life's most pressing challenges haven't arrived because it simply didn't have enough "faith fuel" and ran out of gas?

The vehicle of God's power is able to travel wherever it needs to be. It can take us wherever we need to go. God's power is unstoppable, but I believe it runs on the fuel of our faith. The more you lean on God, the further His power will take you. The more you depend on God, the greater the potential for miracles in your life. The deeper you place your trust in God, the bigger the mountains He can move out of your way. God's power runs on the fuel of our faith. So how far is your faith taking you? Why not increase your dependence on God? Deepen your trust in God. Strengthen your faith in God – and watch God take you farther than you ever imagined you could go.

PERSONAL REFLECTION:

Where are the areas in your life where you have stopped believing? Are you open to taking the chance to believe for a miracle in those areas again?

_____

_____

_____

_____

Does your faith have a breaking point? Are there areas where you refuse to believe?

_____

_____

_____

_____

If there is an area of your life where you have quit believing, how do you plan to resurrect your faith?

_____

_____

_____

_____

Who am I praying for?

_____

_____

_____

_____

What am I praying about?

_____

_____

_____

_____

PRAYER STARTER:
Faithful Father, I thank You because when I have given up on You, You have never given up on me. I thank You for Your consistency and Your faithfulness toward me in every area of my life. Please forgive me for all of the times when I have stopped believing in You. Help me today…

– Amen

Day 18

Can I Explain?

"Gird up now thy loins like a man; for I will demand of thee, and answer thou me." Job 38:3

God doesn't have to explain. He expects us to trust Him. Job wanted an explanation. If I were in his shoes, I'd want one too.

Job had just endured unimaginable trauma and untold calamity... and that's just at the beginning of his story! Having dealt with more mess than most of us could imagine experiencing across multiple lifetimes, I was expecting Job's reaction to be, well... different. I was expecting more anger. More impatience. I expected Job to be more like me.

You see, had I been the writer, the story would read very differently. My responses to my friends' accusations wouldn't have been so thoughtful. My complaints wouldn't have been so measured. I would have been hysterical, and I would have been well within my right. Instead, Job is forlorn, fatigued and frustrated, but never really out of line. He never really goes too far. He does, however, want an explanation.

Seems reasonable, doesn't it? I mean, if anyone has earned an explanation, it's Job. He's gone through the worst and made it look easy. He's taken a beating and kept his chin up and his shoulders squared. He has been a good soldier. He is to be commended. He should get his explanation. He deserves it.

Job does what any reasonable person in his situation would do. He asks for the reasons as to why all of this is happening. Job gets what no reasonable person in his predicament would expect – Job gets nothing. No backstory. No behind the scenes.

No comfort. No explanation. Nothing.

In my opinion, an explanation would have been common courtesy. Not only that, but an explanation would have also helped. At least, it would have helped me. After all, isn't trouble easier when it's explained? Aren't heartaches easier when we know why? Isn't death more palatable when we have a cause? The pain doesn't go away, but it's muted just a little bit when we know where to point the fingers. It hurts a little less when we can figure out who gets the blame.

Job doesn't get any of that. Job gets no explanation at all. As a matter of fact, all Job really gets is a response that shapes up to be basically the opposite of what Job was asking for. In Job chapter 38 God begins a response to Job which can be summed up in the phrase, "Because I said so". That's not an explanation at all! But it does sound familiar.

I'm not proud of it, but I've done it to my kids and my parents did it to me. After a barrage of questions and answers that have been judged insufficient by inquiring little minds, nearly every parent has retreated to the safety of "Because I said so". That means I'm not having this conversation any longer. There will be no further justification, no further explanation. These are the facts, and this is the reality. Even if I could take the time to explain my rationale, you wouldn't really understand. So as your father I'm going to call the shots and you are going to follow instructions. You're doing whatever I've asked you to do... because I said so. We've all been there and done that, and it's been done to all of us.

You see, there comes a time in our faith journey when the explanations we seek are beyond our comprehension, outside of the realm of our responsibilities and frankly, above our pay grade. Yes, it's your life, but it's God's world and God's will. God reserves the right to make decisions without first clearing them with you. If God needed your permission before every trial, then He wouldn't be in charge. If God had to submit an explanation for every challenging situation then He would no longer be the sovereign God. He is in control. He rules and reigns over all our circumstances and remains God in spite of it all. He is King of Kings and Lord of Lords and sometimes things happen just because He said so. And that's ok.

God owes no explanation, but God promises salvation. His intentions are good, so we can trust Him. His heart is love, so we can depend on Him. He knows all, so we can follow Him. Even if He never explains His ways, I can put my trust in His heart. He is a good God, after all.

PERSONAL REFLECTION:
Have you ever argued with God? What was the argument about?
What was the resolution?

_____

_____

_____

Have you ever sought an explanation for anything that God has
allowed? Have you ever received the explanation you sought?

_____

_____

_____

_____

If God explains His actions to you, do you think you would
be able to understand them? Would you always approve? How
would an explanation from God change your relationship with
Him?

_____

_____

_____

_____

Who am I praying for?

_____

_____

_____

What am I praying about?

_____

_____

_____

PRAYER STARTER:
Faithful Father, I thank You for always being patient with me even when I do not understand. I am humbled that You would allow me to express my frustrations and yet show Your love for me through it all. Forgive me for sometimes allowing my frustration and confusion to get the best of me. I ask You today...

_____

_____

_____

_____

_____

_____

_____

_____

_____

_____

_____

_____

_____

_____

_____

_____

_____

_____

_____

_____

– Amen

Day 19

He Knows

*"Declaring the end from the beginning, and from
ancient times the things that are not yet done, saying,
My counsel shall stand, and I will do all my pleasure:"
Isaiah 46:10*

I came across a quote recently that seemed to jump off of my screen and grab me. It definitely got my attention. The quote said, "Everything is figureoutable". It caught me, not just because of a mere word, but because on the surface it sounded true. It sounds like the kind of statement we would all retweet. It represents to me the resilience and resourcefulness we look for in our heroes. Quotes like this make us believe. They make us believe that with enough creativity and enough ingenuity and enough guts and grit, any mountain can be climbed, any river can be crossed, and any problem can be solved. I read a quote like that and I am inspired! Any challenge can be met. Everything is figureoutable! No matter what it is, it can be done. No matter where it is, it can be reached. The challenge might seem confusing, feel overwhelming, and invincible but in the end, it can be figured out.

There are parts of me that wants, no… Needs that to be true. I need to believe in the power of my possibilities and promises of my tomorrows. I need to believe that I'm never hopeless and never helpless. There is the other part of me however, that holds up this quote and this idea to the light of reality, and sees this idea with all of its flaws. You might call that the cynical part. You might call that the doubting part. Call it whatever you want… but it's there in me and it's there in all of us. There's the part that believes that every problem has a solution. Then there's the other part that whispers, "Not so fast."

The "other" part. That's the part that confronts you in the doctor's office when the doctor informs you that you don't have much longer to live. That's the part that sits beside you as you fill out the bankruptcy paperwork and wonder how you will ever be able to pick up the pieces and begin again. That's the part that walks with you into the funeral home to make arrangements for your loved one. Arrangements you never thought you would have had to make because you serve a God that hears and answers your prayers. The "other part" is the part that reminds us of the limits. Medicine can only do so much. Therapy can only go so far. Savings can only cover a certain amount. Friends can only stay but so long. There are some things that can't be fixed. There are some things we just can't figure out.

Turns out we don't know everything. Our experience is limited. Our energy is finite. Our resources are small. Our knowledge is insufficient and incomplete. Our problems are bigger than we are. Our challenges are more complex than we give them credit for. We try, and we make progress but there will always be something just beyond our reach. There are some things we just can't figure out, but thankfully we don't have to. The beauty of our faith lies in the fact that we don't have to figure everything out because we have a Heavenly Father who already knows it all and has already solved it all. He has it all figured out.

The Christian life doesn't require us to have all the answers, it simply requires us to place our faith in the hands of a God that does. God knows the end from the beginning. God has the solution to every problem. God has already figured it out! Let Him lead you. Let Him guide you. Indeed, "Everything is figureoutable" when you place your trust in Him.

PERSONAL REFLECTION:

Where are the confusing areas in your life? How difficult is it to trust God with the stuff that you have not yet figured out?

_____

_____

_____

_____

Do you ever get frustrated facing problems that you cannot solve? How do you deal with them as a person of faith?

_____

_____

_____

_____

In your opinion, what is the difference between trust and apathy? How do you turn your problems over to Jesus while remaining engaged in tackling life's difficult challenges?

_____

_____

_____

_____

Who am I praying for?

_____

_____

_____

_____

What am I praying about?

_____

_____

_____

_____

PRAYER STARTER:

Faithful Father, I am grateful that, whatever the circumstance, You have already figured it out. I can trust in Your knowledge and rest in Your power, knowing that You will work all things out for my good. I praise You in spite of my tendency to sometimes doubt. Please forgive me if my human frailties ever cause me to distrust You. Help me today...

– Amen

Day 20

Give God A Little More Time

"Thy daughter is dead: why troublest thou the master any further?" Mark 5:35b

I wonder what life would be like for all of us if we all had more time. Time is a luxury that most of us cannot afford. Me? I feel like I'm always running out of time. There's always one more thing to do. There's always a little bit farther to go. I could use a little more time.

Who couldn't? It's always nice to have a grace period when paying a bill. It's always nice when the teacher extends the deadline for turning in an assignment. It's always welcomed when the plane is delayed just as I'm running late to the airport (Don't judge me). I can always use a little extra time, because time is hard to come by. It is scarce. It is precious. It moves quickly and once it is gone, it cannot be recovered. No wonder we are so careful with our time.

"Wasting time" never sat well with me. It probably never sat well with you either. I don't set out to be demanding, but I do recognize that my time is precious. So is yours. I'd like to know that, at the end of every day I have been productive. I have maximized my time and used the few moments that I have been given to the best of my ability. As such, I try not to use it frivolously. I think twice before giving it away. Yet, some things require time. Some things will not happen instantly. Some things will not take place in the blink of an eye or at a moment's notice. We will all inevitably have to wait. We will all have to be patient, whether we want to or not.

That's hard these days, especially when everything around us is designed to save us time. We don't wait for food to warm or for traffic to flow or for messages to reach around the world. There's always the microwave, the carpool lane, social media and a hundred other gadgets that help us hurry. So that's exactly what we do... we hurry. We move as fast as we can for as long as we can, and we do that as often as we can. From the moment we open our eyes in the morning to the time we close them at night, most of us are in a hurry... and I think we expect God to do the same. We expect God to hurry, but apparently His sense of time is very different than yours and mine. I'm not sure if God owns a cell phone or uses a watch but I am sure that He isn't enslaved by time or intimidated by time or bullied by time in the same way that I am. From what the Bible reveals about time He is above it and beyond it and controls it and is not subject to it at all.

That fact frustrates me to no end.

It would frustrate you too. It would be especially frustrating if you had an emergency and God was in no hurry. It would be frustrating if you felt God should be responding faster and it felt like He was callously dragging His feet and being slow. Imagine yourself having asked Jesus to heal your daughter and then watching Him slowly wade in the direction of your house with a crowd around Him- only to stop because someone touched Him. Are you serious? You're slowing down when I needed you to hurry! And now the news arrives that your daughter is dead. No need to hurry any more. There's no need to, because according to your watch we have run out of time.

This is where the rubber of our faith meets the road of our patience. Can you give God more time? Even when you can't afford it? Even when it's not comfortable or convenient, can you give God more time? Can you pray again even in your darkest hour? Can you believe again after the deadline has passed and the opportunity has faded, and they've told you that you are way too old? When you are in a hurry and God says, "Be patient", can you give God a little more time?

Faith says keep following Jesus even when the crowd around you says there's no need to bother Him anymore. And you must still follow. Why? You follow because God has a way of turning our endings into new beginnings. We still follow because God can extend deadlines and get past obstacles and get around final notices. We still follow because God can make a way out of no way. As the well-known song says, "He may not come when you want Him, but He's always right on time." We follow because God is never late, our expectations are simply premature.

Follow God. Be patient with His dealings. Give Him just a little more time.

PERSONAL REFLECTION:

Have you ever tried to move God ahead of God's schedule? When God did not hurry, how did you feel?

_____

_____

_____

_____

When was the last time that your schedule and God's schedule did not coincide? What do you do when your timing does not match God's?

_____

_____

_____

_____

What is one area in your life where you need to be more patient with God? Describe what patience will look like.

_____

_____

_____

_____

Who am I praying for?

_____

_____

_____

What am I praying about?

_____

_____

_____

_____

PRAYER STARTER:

Faithful Father, although I am not always patient with You, You are always patient with me and for that, I thank You. I especially thank You for the times when You were patient with me even after I complained. Please forgive me for trying Your patience over and over again. Today I pray...

– Amen

Day 21

What He Sees

"And I will make of thee a great nation, and I will bless thee, and make thy name great; and thou shalt be a blessing." Genesis 12:2

Indulge me for a moment as I take a trip down memory lane. One of the last things my mother asked me to do before she died was, "Write a book." Of course, I ignored her (like any good son is supposed to do!) It seemed premature and somewhat pretentious at the time for me to be writing anything. Honestly, I didn't think I had much of anything to say. I even remembered asking her why she was wasting her time trying to convince me to write a book when in fact, I had other things I should have been doing, but mom persisted, as mothers do. I'm thinking about her now as I am finishing this manuscript. Believe it or not, I did in fact, write a book! Apparently, mom saw something in me that at the time I did not see in myself. To me, what she saw did not exist. I was skeptical because what she identified at the time just was not there. At least, it wasn't there from what I could tell. For the life of me I could not see myself writing. For her, the vision was as plain as day. Now that one of her many dreams has become reality I am looking at my work and wishing she could read it. No doubt she'd tell everybody who would listen that her son wrote not one, but two books. I think she would be proud. I'm also looking at the manuscript and wondering how she knew. How could she look so far ahead and be correct in identifying what she saw? How could she look so deep inside and determine that potential was present that I could not see?

You probably answered, "Because she was your mother". I'm

really happy for you. Imma let you finish... (Why is that still shocking AND entertaining ten years later? If you don't know what I'm talking about, google it. Thank me later.) Anyway, consider this: There are plenty of moms and dads out there who have never recognized or identified the potential of their children. Once upon a time, I used to substitute teach in a public school in Washington, D.C. Now maybe this wouldn't strike you as surprising at all, but I was shocked at just how many parents expected absolutely nothing from their children. It's one thing for the students to have no vision, no expectations, no dreams and no goals. Maybe they haven't been taught. Maybe they haven't been exposed. Maybe they haven't been nurtured. Maybe they don't know any better. The parents, however? That is a different story. That is what threw me for a loop. You would think that the parents would know better. You'd think that the parents would do better. Yet, here were parents who were not even slightly bothered that their little bundles of joy were doing painfully bad in the classroom. It was as if some of these underachievers came from parents who expected them to fail! They saw nothing in their children except for the same disappointment and failure that has plagued their lives. It was incredibly sad to walk out of that school week after week knowing that those expectations of failure from those parents might well one day become self-fulfilling prophecies.

There was potential in every one of those children. Those around them didn't always see it. In each one of those chairs sat an untapped genius with the potential to be an engineer, pilot, teacher, dentist, nurse, musician, minister, or anything else they thought that God was calling them to be. Blank canvases sat in the classroom every day just waiting to be covered in encouragement. Empty vessels sat behind each desk waiting for greatness to be poured within. So many bright futures didn't have the benefit of a home that saw the potential for any kind of light at all. Greatness was there, but many came from homes where those who raised them just could not see.

Not every parent is a Richard Williams who places a tennis racket in Venus and Serena's hands when they could barely walk much less hit a ball- just because they see the greatness. Not every parent is an Earl Woods who put a golf club in young Tiger's hand by the time he was two years old because he could see the greatness. Moms and dads all hear the same things "Your child could change the world" Not everyone believes it. Parents are all told about the untapped potential. Not everybody sees it.

It takes special vision to see what doesn't yet exist and what others don't think is even there. Maybe that's why it's hard for us to have faith in each other. Faith is the evidence of things not seen, and many of us can't see past the nose on our faces much less see the magic stuff in others that has yet to materialize… but God can. God can see the potential inside of you because He put it there. God can see the best in you because He created you. God can see greatness because He implanted it within you, and He wants desperately for you to trust Him so that He can bring it out.

God sees what our parents occasionally could not see. God sees what our teachers sometimes couldn't believe was ever there. God sees the dreams that the detractors and the distractors try to discredit and destroy before they ever come to pass. God sees it all because He knows what He placed inside. He knows you. He knows me. He loves us, and we can trust Him. We can trust what He's planned. We can trust what He knows. We can follow Him. We can trust what He sees.

PERSONAL REFLECTION:
How do you think the potential God sees within you sometimes conflicts with what you see within yourself?

_____

_____

_____

_____

Do you have any underutilized talents? List one below. Now take time to celebrate this area of potential that God has placed within you.

_____

_____

_____

_____

Consider one thing you would accomplish if failure were not a possibility. What is stopping you from realizing that dream?

_____

_____

_____

_____

Who am I praying for?

_____

_____

_____

What am I praying about?

_____

_____

_____

PRAYER STARTER:
Faithful Father, I thank You for seeing things in me that I do not acknowledge are even there. Even in my darkest hours, You see the best in me always and for that I am grateful. Forgive me for the times I have not lived up to what You have in store for me. Help me today....

– Amen

ABOUT THE AUTHOR

Gamal T. Alexander is a passionate storyteller whose mission is to help others communicate more effectively while himself telling the story of Jesus' love. Born in Brooklyn, NY and raised in Raleigh, NC, he now lives in Southern California where he pastors the Compton Community Church. He coaches, speaks, and writes regularly while traveling across the country. He is the father of two daughters, Faith and Grace. You can find out more about Gamal by visiting www.gamalalexander.com.

CPSIA information can be obtained
at www.ICGtesting.com
Printed in the USA
FSHW022017310819
61594FS